Leif
the
Lucky

Also by Ingri and Edgar Parin d'Aulaire
Published by the University of Minnesota Press

Children of the Northlights
Ola

LEIF THE LUCKY

by INGRI & EDGAR PARIN D'AULAIRE

University of Minnesota Press
Minneapolis · London

Publisher's Note

The term *Skraellinger* was used by Norse explorers to describe the Indigenous people of North America. This word is not appropriate today. Our knowledge and appreciation of Indigenous peoples and cultures have advanced significantly since this book was first published. To remain faithful to the authors' language and contribute to Scandinavian American literary heritage, *Leif the Lucky* is reprinted here in its original form, but we encourage readers to recognize the essential changes to language and historical accounts that now treat Indigenous peoples with greater accuracy and respect.

The University of Minnesota Press gratefully acknowledges assistance provided for the publication of this book by the John K. and Elsie Lampert Fesler Fund.

Originally published in 1941 by Doubleday, Doran & Company, Inc.

First University of Minnesota Press edition, 2014

Published by the University of Minnesota Press
111 Third Avenue South, Suite 290
Minneapolis, MN 55401-2520
http://www.upress.umn.edu

Library of Congress Cataloging-in-Publication Data
D'Aulaire, Ingri, 1904–1980. D'Aulaire, Edgar Parin, 1898–1986.
    Leif the Lucky / Ingri and Edgar Parin d'Aulaire. — First University of Minnesota Press edition.
    ISBN 978-0-8166-9545-4 (hc : acid-free paper)
    1. Leiv Eiriksson—approximately 1020—Juvenile literature. 2. Explorers—America—Biography—Juvenile literature. 3. Explorers—Norway—Biography—Juvenile literature. 4. America—Discovery and exploration—Norse—Juvenile literature. 5. Vikings—Juvenile literature. I. D'Aulaire, Edgar Parin, 1898–1986, joint author. II. Title.
    E105.L47D38 2014
    973.1'3092—dc23 [B]
                                                                    2014009179

Printed in China on acid-free paper

The University of Minnesota is an equal-opportunity educator and employer.

29 28 27 26 25 24   12 11 10 9 8

A THOUSAND YEARS AGO when the Vikings roamed the seas, led by their Norse gods, there lived a man in Norway called Erik the Red. He was able and strong but his temper was wild, and after a fight he was banned from Norway. So he sailed to Iceland. There he built a farm, found a wife, and lived in peace for a while. But then he began to quarrel and fight again, and it wasn't long before he had to flee from Iceland, too. Now Erik sailed off into the unknown sea toward the setting sun, and there behind a wall of ice he found a new land. Eternal ice and snow covered most of the land, but the banks of the fjords were green with grass. No men, no houses he found, but on the edge of the ice lay sleek seals and snoring walruses. And polar bears, foxes, and hares hurried silently, like shadows, over the icy wastes. This seemed to Erik a good land for fierce Vikings who kept their peace best when far away from neighbors. He sailed back to Iceland for his wife and his sons, and after his friends had listened for a while to his stories of the vast and green lands he had found, many decided to move there with him.

Erik the Red had three sons. The one was called Torstein, the second Torvald, and the third was called Leif. And this is the story of Leif, Erik's son, who sailed with his father to Greenland and who later sailed still farther west and found there the continent of America.

Leif stood on sturdy feet in the prow of his father's Viking ship as he sailed across the Snowstorm Sea. The brine stung his tanned cheeks and the wind tore at his hair. His eyes were keen as the eyes of a snake and blue as steel as he watched the rows of waves rising like a thousand fences between him and his new home in the West.

Leif's father, Erik the Red, stood at the rudder himself and steered his ship with his huge fists. He led the way for twenty-four ships that sailed after him as he sailed ahead. For twenty-four chieftains were moving with him to the

new land he had found. On all the ships there was a great squeeze of people and cattle and fodder and food. On Erik's ship were his wife and his children, his servants and thralls, and everything that belonged to him.

For days they sailed through mountains of waves and through valleys of water, and Leif saw nothing but sea and sky and drifting ice. Then one day he spied far, far away, a mountain sticking out of the sea. Yes! Soon the others saw

it, too, and Erik told Leif to hurry and take the dragon head off the prow of the ship. "For gaping heads and yawning snouts anger the spirits of the land," said Erik. Head over heels Leif climbed up and took off the dragon head.

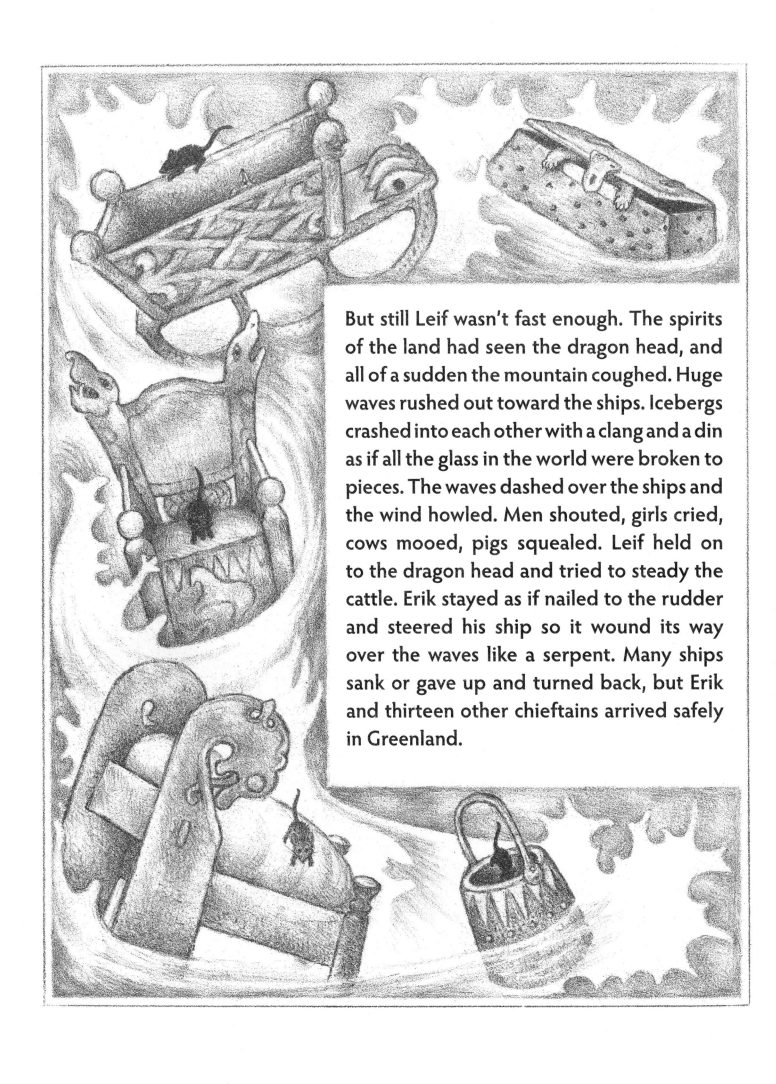

But still Leif wasn't fast enough. The spirits of the land had seen the dragon head, and all of a sudden the mountain coughed. Huge waves rushed out toward the ships. Icebergs crashed into each other with a clang and a din as if all the glass in the world were broken to pieces. The waves dashed over the ships and the wind howled. Men shouted, girls cried, cows mooed, pigs squealed. Leif held on to the dragon head and tried to steady the cattle. Erik stayed as if nailed to the rudder and steered his ship so it wound its way over the waves like a serpent. Many ships sank or gave up and turned back, but Erik and thirteen other chieftains arrived safely in Greenland.

They sailed into a deep fjord and landed at a steep green slope. Trip, trap, trip, trap, down the gangplank people and animals rushed to get their feet on solid ground. "Fair are these slopes and here we shall build," said Erik the Red.

"Fair is the smell of the porridge pot," thought Leif to himself, for they couldn't build a fire to cook any food on the ships. Then they all ate their porridge and drank from the brooks, and the animals grazed on the sunny slopes.

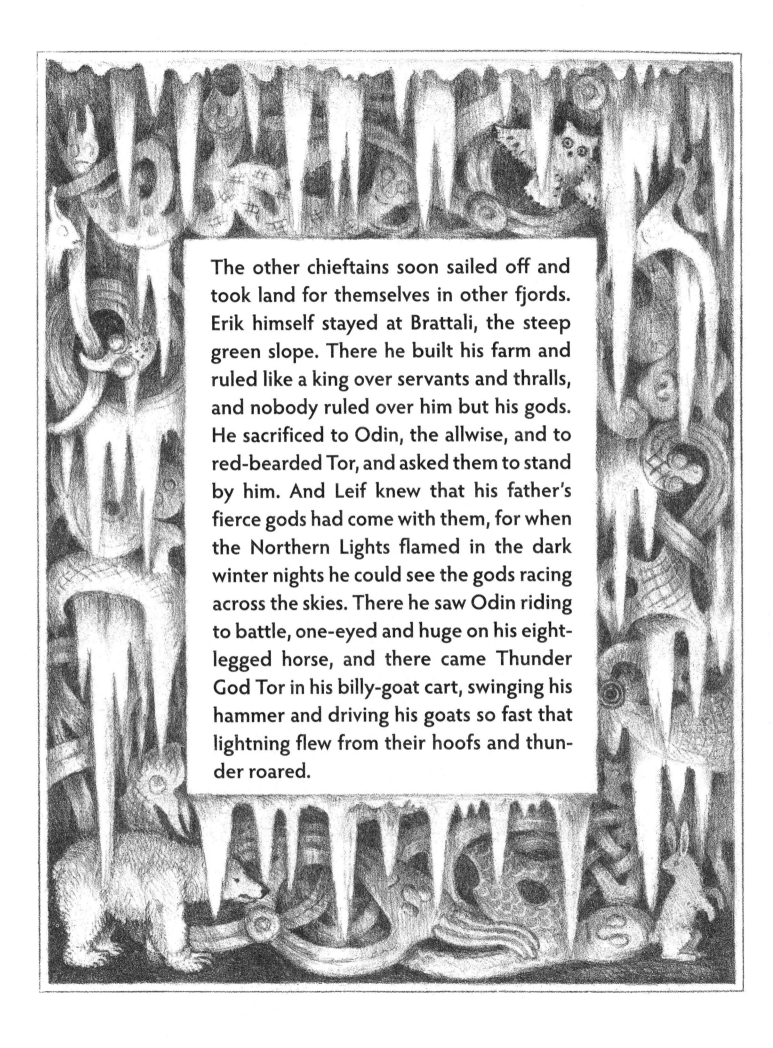

The other chieftains soon sailed off and took land for themselves in other fjords. Erik himself stayed at Brattali, the steep green slope. There he built his farm and ruled like a king over servants and thralls, and nobody ruled over him but his gods. He sacrificed to Odin, the allwise, and to red-bearded Tor, and asked them to stand by him. And Leif knew that his father's fierce gods had come with them, for when the Northern Lights flamed in the dark winter nights he could see the gods racing across the skies. There he saw Odin riding to battle, one-eyed and huge on his eight-legged horse, and there came Thunder God Tor in his billy-goat cart, swinging his hammer and driving his goats so fast that lightning flew from their hoofs and thunder roared.

Leif grew up in Greenland and became strong and cunning as a chieftain's son should be. He sailed his ship, threw his spear, and swung his axe and from his father he learned to be swift as an arrow and quiet as a mouse. He dressed his boat in polar bear skins so that it looked like a chunk of floating ice and went hunting seal and walrus. For hours he sat still and silent at a hole in the ice, waiting for a seal to come up for air. But sometimes he became so excited that he forgot and whispered under his breath: "I'll catch you," and then the seal was gone! When the winter storms soared over the house he played around the fire with a white bear cub. Then he needed all his skill, for the bear was strong and tough, too. And Erik laughed until his stiff frozen beard tinkled like bells when he came home from hunting with a six-man's load on his shoulders.

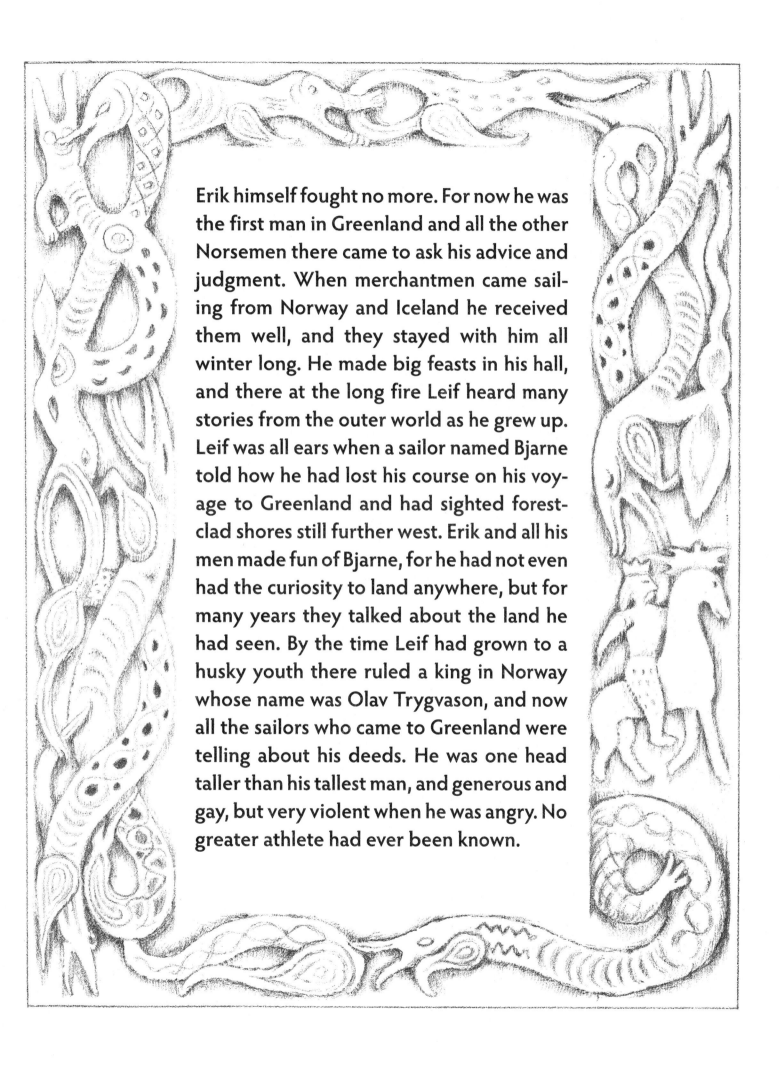

Erik himself fought no more. For now he was the first man in Greenland and all the other Norsemen there came to ask his advice and judgment. When merchantmen came sailing from Norway and Iceland he received them well, and they stayed with him all winter long. He made big feasts in his hall, and there at the long fire Leif heard many stories from the outer world as he grew up. Leif was all ears when a sailor named Bjarne told how he had lost his course on his voyage to Greenland and had sighted forest-clad shores still further west. Erik and all his men made fun of Bjarne, for he had not even had the curiosity to land anywhere, but for many years they talked about the land he had seen. By the time Leif had grown to a husky youth there ruled a king in Norway whose name was Olav Trygvason, and now all the sailors who came to Greenland were telling about his deeds. He was one head taller than his tallest man, and generous and gay, but very violent when he was angry. No greater athlete had ever been known.

He could throw two spears at once, yes, he could play with three swords and run along the blades of the oars while his men rowed the ship. By day and by night Leif dreamed of this glorious king and wanted to sail to his court.

Ships were scarce in Greenland, for there were no woods, but at last Leif got a ship of his own and set out. He sailed straight east to the islands west of Scotland and when fair winds came again he sailed on to Nidaros in Norway.

In Nidaros everything was great and fine. From houses and wharves people watched Leif as he stepped ashore with all his rare gifts for the king. A Greenland falcon perched on his fist, and a white bear cub walked at his heels. Then came his men with homespuns and furs and walrus tusks and ropes of walrus hide so strong that sixty men couldn't tear them apart. Leif went on till he came to the door of the king's hall. There he stopped to comb his hair, and waited till the king had eaten his fill. For thus it was best to approach the king he had learned from his father. In the great hall King Olav sat at table with his men, and he was still handsomer than Leif had thought.

Now it was a strict rule at court that as soon as the king put aside his knife and spoon everyone else had to stop eating too. But there sat at the table a little fat man who was so busy eating he didn't even have time to look up.

When the king saw this offense against his royal rule, he moved his eyebrows up and down in wrath, and all his men turned pale. "He shall eat till he bursts," growled the king, and he ordered his servants to put huge vats of

porridge before the man. "Eat it all up," roared the king. The man ate till his belt buckle burst, his cheeks turned blue, and even his shoelaces flew apart. Then he threw himself on his knees. "Kill me, Sire King, but not with porridge, not with porridge," begged the man. Then King Olav couldn't help laughing, and all his men laughed with him, and the little fat man was spared. Now King Olav noticed Leif standing in the doorway with all his strange gifts, and, highly pleased, he gave him a sign to approach. The king saw at once that Leif was a well-mannered youth and asked him to stay at his court. He showed him great favors, and that winter Leif took part in all the games, and saw for himself all the king's feats that no other man could equal.

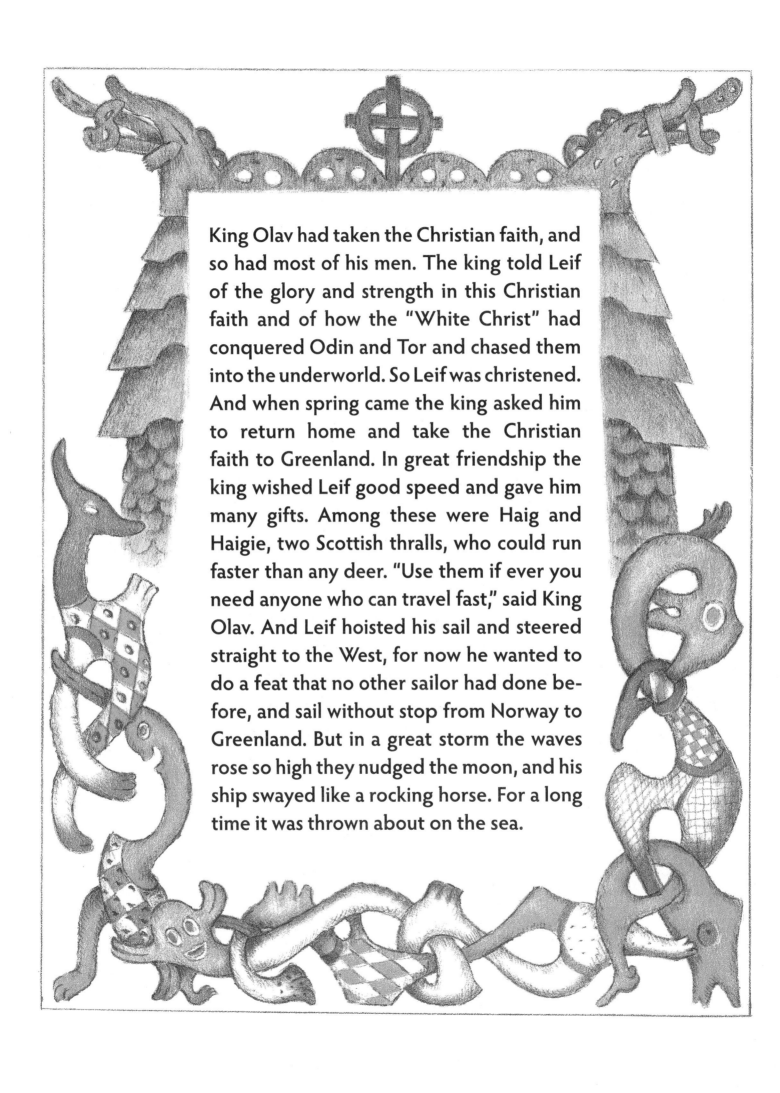

King Olav had taken the Christian faith, and so had most of his men. The king told Leif of the glory and strength in this Christian faith and of how the "White Christ" had conquered Odin and Tor and chased them into the underworld. So Leif was christened. And when spring came the king asked him to return home and take the Christian faith to Greenland. In great friendship the king wished Leif good speed and gave him many gifts. Among these were Haig and Haigie, two Scottish thralls, who could run faster than any deer. "Use them if ever you need anyone who can travel fast," said King Olav. And Leif hoisted his sail and steered straight to the West, for now he wanted to do a feat that no other sailor had done before, and sail without stop from Norway to Greenland. But in a great storm the waves rose so high they nudged the moon, and his ship swayed like a rocking horse. For a long time it was thrown about on the sea.

Then the wind calmed down and a heavy fog fell over them. Leif could see neither whales nor the sun nor the color of the sea to guide his way, but he sailed on, thinking, "If I don't find Greenland maybe I'll find the land that Bjarne saw." At last the fog lifted enough for Leif's keen eyes to pierce it,

and there, straight ahead, he saw land. It was a beautiful land with forests of strange trees growing all the way down to the shores. "No one shall laugh at us as they laughed at Bjarne and say we didn't explore the land," said Leif. So he sailed up to the shore and landed at the mouth of a river.

He sent Haig and Haigie to run over all the hills, and when they came back and said they had seen neither people nor smoke from fires, Leif and his men went ashore and built themselves houses. All through the summer they lived

in great plenty and were carefree and did nothing but enjoy the land, for it was so rich that wild grains and grapevines and all kinds of fruits grew there. And Leif gave the land a name, and called it Vinland or Wineland.

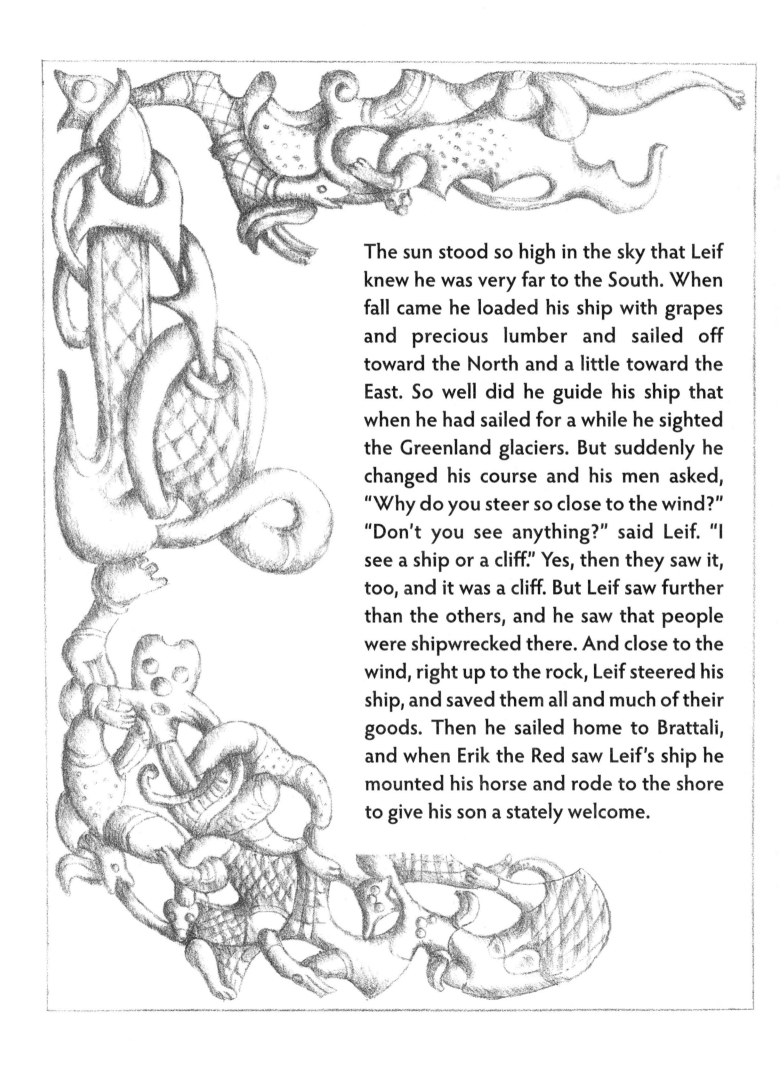

The sun stood so high in the sky that Leif knew he was very far to the South. When fall came he loaded his ship with grapes and precious lumber and sailed off toward the North and a little toward the East. So well did he guide his ship that when he had sailed for a while he sighted the Greenland glaciers. But suddenly he changed his course and his men asked, "Why do you steer so close to the wind?" "Don't you see anything?" said Leif. "I see a ship or a cliff." Yes, then they saw it, too, and it was a cliff. But Leif saw further than the others, and he saw that people were shipwrecked there. And close to the wind, right up to the rock, Leif steered his ship, and saved them all and much of their goods. Then he sailed home to Brattali, and when Erik the Red saw Leif's ship he mounted his horse and rode to the shore to give his son a stately welcome.

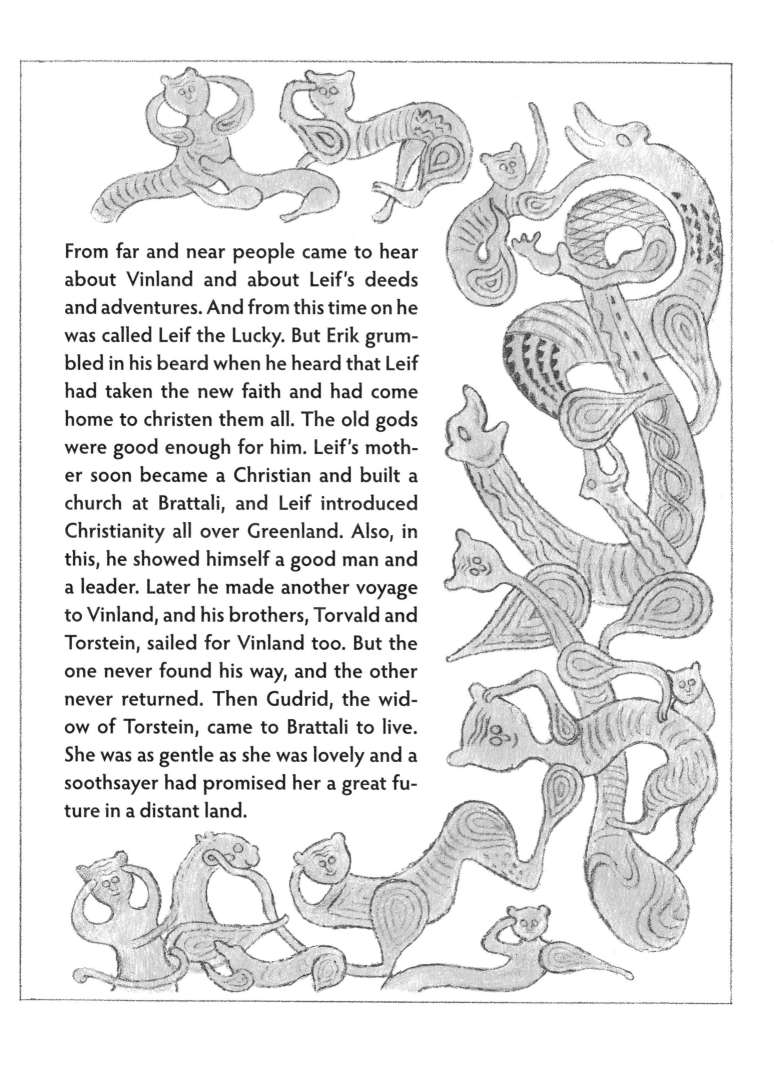

From far and near people came to hear about Vinland and about Leif's deeds and adventures. And from this time on he was called Leif the Lucky. But Erik grumbled in his beard when he heard that Leif had taken the new faith and had come home to christen them all. The old gods were good enough for him. Leif's mother soon became a Christian and built a church at Brattali, and Leif introduced Christianity all over Greenland. Also, in this, he showed himself a good man and a leader. Later he made another voyage to Vinland, and his brothers, Torvald and Torstein, sailed for Vinland too. But the one never found his way, and the other never returned. Then Gudrid, the widow of Torstein, came to Brattali to live. She was as gentle as she was lovely and a soothsayer had promised her a great future in a distant land.

One summer a merchantman called Torfinn Karlsevne came sailing his ship to Brattali. Torfinn soon fell in love with Gudrid, and as he was rich and highborn he was well received when he asked her in marriage. And that winter it was decided that Torfinn and Gudrid should sail to Vinland to make their home there. Leif helped them in every way. He told them how to sail, sent with them some of his sailors and also Haig and Haigie, and said they could use his houses in Vinland. In the spring Torfinn and Gudrid set off. With them sailed two more ships and one hundred and fifty Norsemen with cattle and household goods.

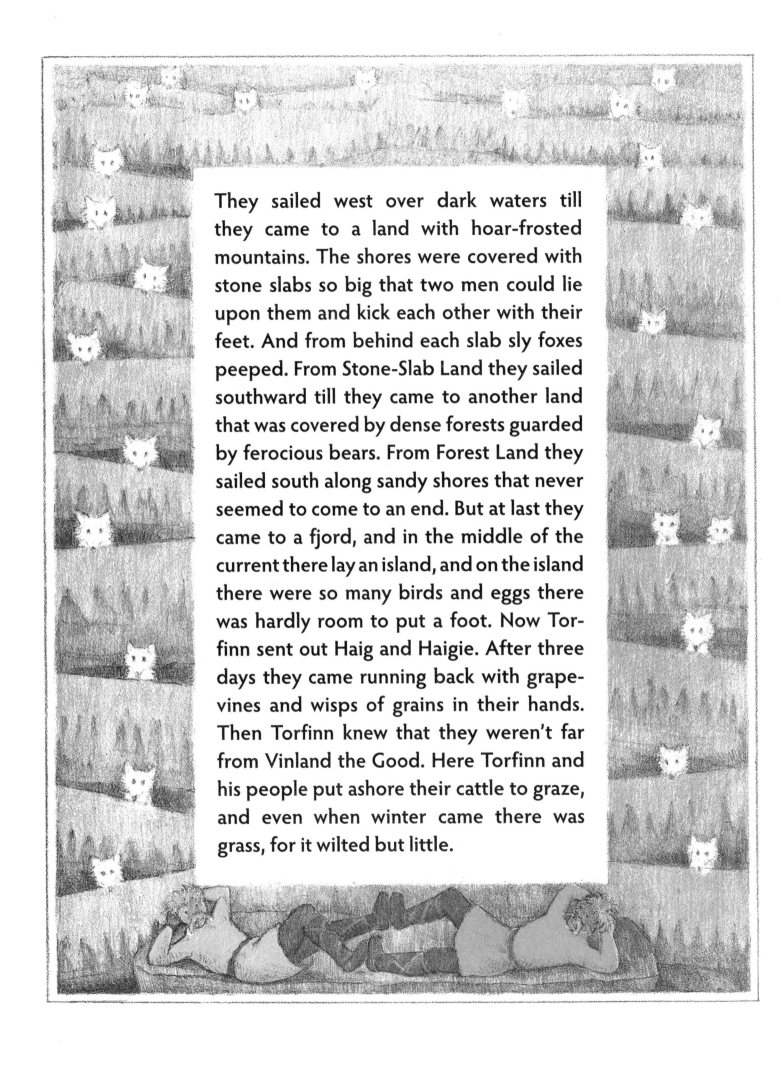

They sailed west over dark waters till they came to a land with hoar-frosted mountains. The shores were covered with stone slabs so big that two men could lie upon them and kick each other with their feet. And from behind each slab sly foxes peeped. From Stone-Slab Land they sailed southward till they came to another land that was covered by dense forests guarded by ferocious bears. From Forest Land they sailed south along sandy shores that never seemed to come to an end. But at last they came to a fjord, and in the middle of the current there lay an island, and on the island there were so many birds and eggs there was hardly room to put a foot. Now Torfinn sent out Haig and Haigie. After three days they came running back with grape-vines and wisps of grains in their hands. Then Torfinn knew that they weren't far from Vinland the Good. Here Torfinn and his people put ashore their cattle to graze, and even when winter came there was grass, for it wilted but little.

That winter a baby boy was born to Gudrid and Torfinn. Torfinn put his son on his knees and named him Snorre, and this Snorre was the first white child ever born in America. When spring came Torfinn led the ships still further south, and now they came to Vinland the Good. Here they all liked it and settled down to live, and Snorre grew big and strong in the sun. But on a fair day when everything was all pleasure and joy, the Norsemen saw a number of skin boats rounding the point to the south. In the boats were dark-skinned people with black and unkempt hair, and they all had sticks in their hands which they whirled to the right. It sounded as if they were threshing. "Maybe this is a sign of peace," said one of Torfinn's men, and the Norsemen held their white shields toward them, for this was their sign of friendship. The natives came ashore and they gazed at each other. Then the natives jumped into their boats and paddled off again.

Skraellinger was what the Norsemen called these people. They saw no more of them for a while. Then the dark men came back in great numbers and wanted to barter fine furs. Gudrid gave them clabber and cream and cheese and butter, and they licked their fingers and traded beautiful furs for this milk food

they had never tasted before. Torfinn had brought big balls of red cloth. He cut it up into narrow strips and traded it, a foot for each fur. The Skraellinger all wanted red cloth, so when there was little left, he cut it up into finger-wide strips, and for a foot of this he got just as much fur, yes, even more.

When all the cloth was gone the Norsemen had great heaps of furs. And the Skraellinger strutted about wrapped in red ribbons. Now Torfinn had a big bull that was grazing in the woods, and the sight of all the red cloth must have made the bull angry. For all of a sudden, with a roar and a bellow, he charged straight for the Skraellinger. The Skraellinger, who had never seen a bull before, jumped and ran and raced for their boats. And much offended they paddled away. Torfinn and his men laughed till they fell on their backs.

But they didn't laugh when three weeks later the Skraellinger came paddling back in such great numbers that it looked as if coals were strewn on the water. Now they all yelled and whirled their sticks fiercely to the left. Then the Norsemen grasped their red shields and ran to meet them in battle. For they weren't men to shun a fight whatever the numbers against them. The Skraellinger leaped from their boats and slung something huge and black toward the Norsemen. It looked like a black ball, or rather more like a giant sheep's belly. It hissed over their heads and came down among them with a terrible crash. This didn't seem natural to the Norsemen. A great fear came over them and they turned and ran. But now it seemed that even the trees were turning into Skraellinger wherever they ran. The Norsemen were spellbound and confused, but the women were not. They urged their men to fight. And when the Skraellinger saw a Viking woman sharpening a sword on her own skin, they in turn were startled and fled.

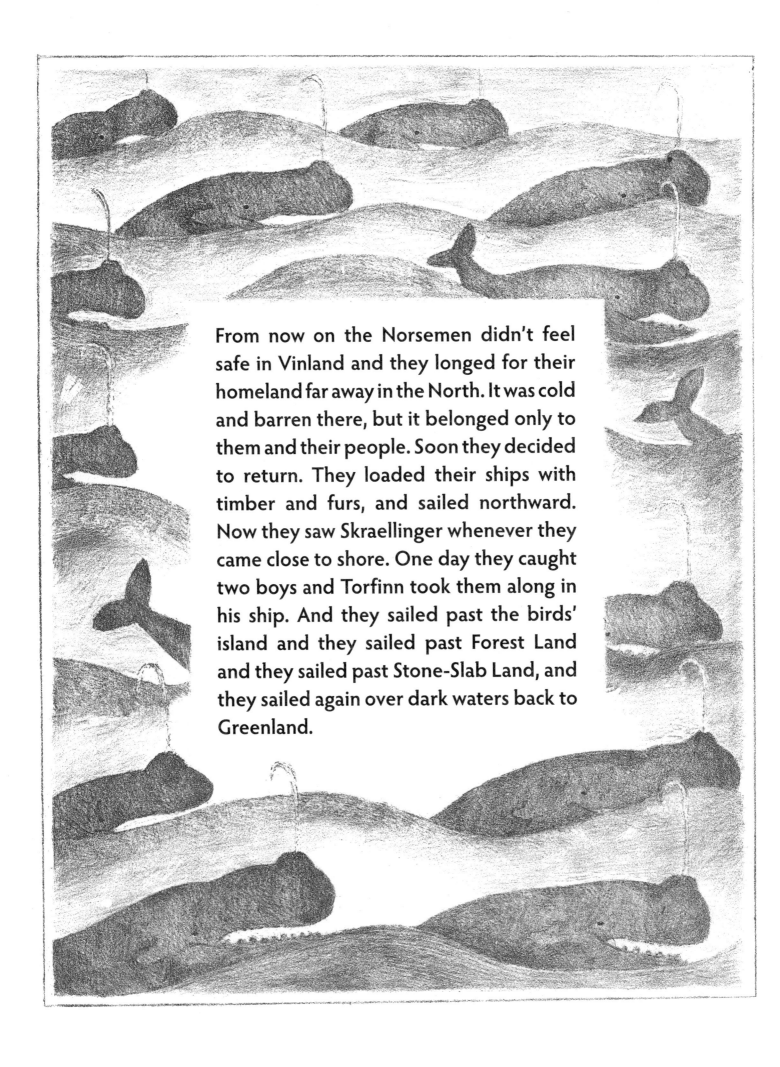

From now on the Norsemen didn't feel safe in Vinland and they longed for their homeland far away in the North. It was cold and barren there, but it belonged only to them and their people. Soon they decided to return. They loaded their ships with timber and furs, and sailed northward. Now they saw Skraellinger whenever they came close to shore. One day they caught two boys and Torfinn took them along in his ship. And they sailed past the birds' island and they sailed past Forest Land and they sailed past Stone-Slab Land, and they sailed again over dark waters back to Greenland.

And while the ice closed in around Greenland and locked it away from the rest of
the world, they all sat together again in
the smoke-filled hall on Brattali. Leif sat
in the high seat now, for Erik the Red had
died, old and full of days. And Leif played
with Snorre, and listened to the Vinland
stories. The two Skraellinger boys soon
learned the language, and they told many
stories about their people. They had no
houses, they said, but lived in holes and
dens, and were ruled by two kings who
were called Avalldamon and Valdidida.
The Norsemen all agreed that the natives
made the new lands too dangerous to live
in. But it would be good to send ships
there for timber as the voyage to Vinland
and Forest Land was much shorter than
that to Norway.

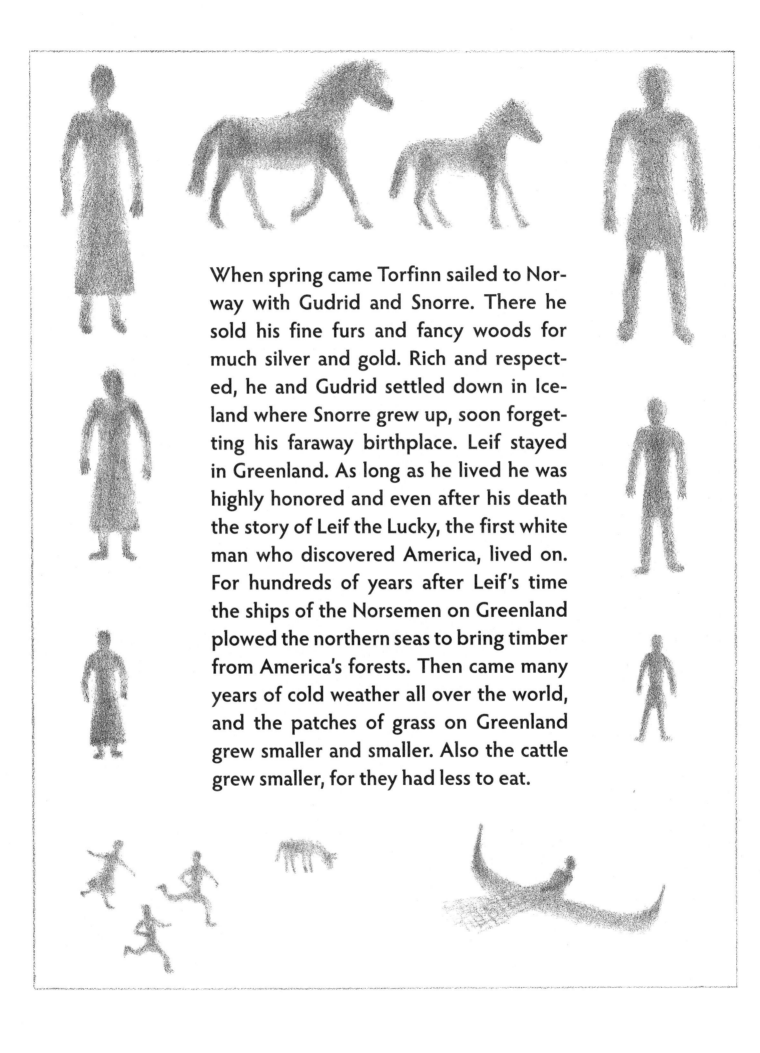

When spring came Torfinn sailed to Norway with Gudrid and Snorre. There he sold his fine furs and fancy woods for much silver and gold. Rich and respected, he and Gudrid settled down in Iceland where Snorre grew up, soon forgetting his faraway birthplace. Leif stayed in Greenland. As long as he lived he was highly honored and even after his death the story of Leif the Lucky, the first white man who discovered America, lived on. For hundreds of years after Leif's time the ships of the Norsemen on Greenland plowed the northern seas to bring timber from America's forests. Then came many years of cold weather all over the world, and the patches of grass on Greenland grew smaller and smaller. Also the cattle grew smaller, for they had less to eat.

The horses became as small as ponies and the cows became almost as small as goats. Even the tall Norsemen grew smaller. The son became smaller than his father, and his son became smaller again, for they had neither porridge nor bread to eat. As they grew smaller they also lost their skill and forgot how to make sturdy, sea-going ships. Without good ships they could neither sail to Norway for food nor to America for timber to build new ships. And at last they had only small boats made of skin for fishing in the Greenland fjords. Soon everybody had forgotten about the Norsemen in Greenland. And several hundred years later when sailors from Norway again came to Greenland they found no Norsemen but in their place squat-legged Eskimos waddling in the ice and snow.

Though this story of Leif the Lucky was written down in old manuscripts, nobody read them for hundreds of years. As the Norsemen in Greenland were forgotten, so were the stories of Vinland. And still for many hundred years the Indians in America could enjoy their land in peace.

Ingri & Edgar Parin d'Aulaire WILTON CONN

Known for their vibrant and imaginative interpretations of Scandinavian folklore, Greek and Norse mythology, and American history, the books of **Ingri** (1904–1980) and **Edgar Parin d'Aulaire** (1898–1986) have entertained readers for more than seventy-five years. The couple made frequent trips to Norway, where they gathered inspiration for many of their most celebrated books, including *Children of the Northlights* (Minnesota, 2012), *East of the Sun and West of the Moon, d'Aulaires' Book of Norse Myths, d'Aulaires' Book of Trolls,* and *Ola* (Minnesota, 2013). The d'Aulaires received the Caldecott Medal in 1940 for their book *Abraham Lincoln* and were later awarded the Regina Medal for their distinguished contribution to children's literature.